MW01051676

ANCHOR
COLORING BOOK

Get FREE printable coloring pages and discounted book prices sent straight to your e-mail inbox every week!

Sign up at:
www.adultcoloringworld.net

ISBN-13: 978-1530726820
ISBN-10: 1530726824

PREVIEWS:

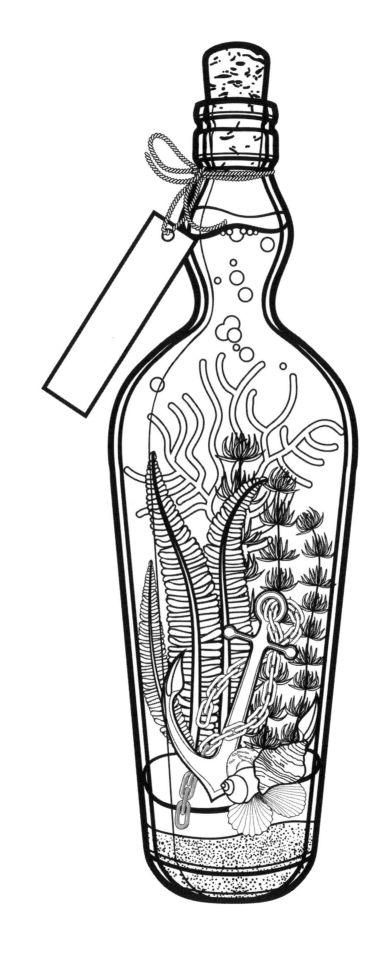

COLOR TEST PAGE

COLOR TEST PAGE

Made in the USA
Middletown, DE
28 December 2018